The List Advantage: Unlocking the Power of List Building for Marketing Success

B. Vincent

Published by RWG Publishing, 2023.

While every precaution has been taken in the preparation of this book, the publisher assumes no responsibility for errors or omissions, or for damages resulting from the use of the information contained herein.

THE LIST ADVANTAGE: UNLOCKING THE POWER OF LIST BUILDING FOR MARKETING SUCCESS

First edition. April 12, 2023.

Copyright © 2023 B. Vincent.

Written by B. Vincent.

Also by B. Vincent

Affiliate Marketing
Affiliate Marketing
Affiliate Marketing

Standalone
Business Employee Discipline
Affiliate Recruiting
Business Layoffs & Firings
Business and Entrepreneur Guide
Business Remote Workforce
Career Transition
Project Management
Precision Targeting
Professional Development
Strategic Planning
Content Marketing
Imminent List Building
Getting Past GateKeepers
Banner Ads
Bookkeeping
Bridge Pages
Business Acquisition

Business Bogging
Business Communication Course
Marketing Automation
Better Meetings
Business Conflict Resolution
Business Culture Course
Conversion Optimization
Creative Solutions
Employee Recruitment
Startup Capital
Employee Incentives
Employee Mentoring
Followership
Servant Leadership
Human Resources
Team Building
Freelancing
Funnel Building
Geo Targeting
Goal Setting
Immanent List Building
Lead Generation
Leadership Course
Leadership Transition
Leadership vs Management
LinkedIn Ads
LinkedIn Marketing
Messenger Marketing
New Management
Newsfeed Ads
Search Ads
Online Learning
Sales Webinars

Side Hustles
Split Testing
Twitter Timeline Advertising
Earning Additional Income Through Side Hustles: Begin Earning Money Immediately
Making a Living Through Blogging: Earn Money Working From Home
Create Bonuses for Affiliate Marketing: Your Success Is Encompassed by Your Bonuses
Internet Marketing Success: The Most Effective Traffic-Driving Strategies
JV Recruiting: Joint Ventures Partnerships and Affiliates
Secrets to List Building
Step-by-Step Facebook Marketing: Discover How To Create A Strategy That Will Help You Grow Your Business
Banner Advertising: Traffic Can Be Boosted by Banner Ads
Affiliate Marketing
Improve Your Marketing Strategy with Internet Marketing
Outsourcing Helps You Save Time and Money
Choosing the Right Content and Marketing for Social Media
Make Products That Will Sell
Launching a Product for Affiliate Marketing
Pinterest as a Marketing Tool
The List Advantage: Unlocking the Power of List Building for Marketing Success

Table of Contents

Chapter 1: The Power of List Building in Modern Marketing 1
Chapter 2: Understanding the Basics of List Building 3
Chapter 3: The Different Types of Lists and Their Benefits 7
Chapter 4: Building a High-Quality Email List from Scratch 11
Chapter 5: Maximizing Your Lead Magnet Strategy for List Building 15
Chapter 6: Crafting Effective Opt-In Forms and Landing Pages . 19
Chapter 7: The Anatomy of an Effective Welcome Email 23
Chapter 8: Creating Killer Content to Build Your List 27
Chapter 9: The Importance of Segmentation and Personalization 31
Chapter 10: Developing a Winning Email Marketing Strategy ... 35
Chapter 11: Mastering the Art of Email Copywriting 39
Chapter 12: A/B Testing Your Emails for Optimal Results 43
Chapter 13: Automating Your List Building and Email Marketing 47
Chapter 14: The Role of Social Media in List Building 51
Chapter 15: Using Influencer Marketing to Build Your List 55
Chapter 16: Harnessing the Power of Referral Marketing 59
Chapter 17: Creating a Sense of Urgency to Encourage Sign-Ups 63
Chapter 18: The Benefits of Offering Lead Magnets and Freebies 67
Chapter 19: How to Measure the Success of Your List Building Efforts 71
Chapter 20: Staying Compliant with Email Marketing Regulations 75
Chapter 21: Nurturing Your Subscribers and Building Trust 79
Chapter 22: Leveraging Analytics to Improve Your List Building 83
Chapter 23: Tapping into the Power of Mobile List Building 87

Chapter 24: The Benefits of List Building for E-commerce Businesses..91

Chapter 25: Implementing List Building for B2B Marketing Success 95

Chapter 26: Scaling Your List Building Efforts for Rapid Growth..99

Chapter 27: Overcoming Common List Building Challenges.. 103

Chapter 28: The Future of List Building and Email Marketing 107

Chapter 1: The Power of List Building in Modern Marketing

Even in this day and age, when social media and other online platforms have taken over the marketing landscape, list building is still a powerful tool that companies can use to connect with their customers and build awareness of their brand. List building is the process of gathering email addresses and other contact information from prospective clients who have shown interest in your product or service. This information can include names, phone numbers, and addresses. After that, these email addresses are added to your email list, which you can then use to communicate with your subscribers and send them content that is informative as well as promotional.

There are a great number of advantages to list building. To begin, it enables companies to communicate directly with their customers, which can be especially helpful for companies operating in specialized markets or for those operating in small businesses. You will be able to cultivate a more meaningful relationship with your customers and maintain their interest in your brand if you have direct access to their email inboxes.

In addition to this, list building is a cost-effective method of marketing your goods and services to potential customers. List building enables businesses to send targeted messages to individuals who have already indicated an interest in what the company has to offer, in contrast to more conventional advertising methods such as commercials broadcast on television or radio. Because of this, creating a list is a method that is both more efficient and effective in reaching potential customers.

In addition, the process of building customer lists gives businesses a great deal of control over the marketing efforts they undertake. Businesses can construct and maintain their own email lists, eliminating the need to rely on third-party platforms to promote their wares. They have full control over the messaging, timing, and frequency of their marketing campaigns as a result of this.

Building a list is a great way to increase both customer loyalty and the credibility of your brand. You can establish yourself as an authority in your field and build trust with your audience if you give your subscribers content that is of value to them. This has the potential to result in higher conversion rates as well as increased customer loyalty.

In conclusion, building mailing lists is an adaptable marketing strategy that can be tailored to meet the requirements of any company, regardless of its size or sector of operation. Building a customer mailing list can be beneficial to the expansion of a company of any size, from a fledgling startup to an established multinational conglomerate.

In conclusion, list building is a potent marketing tool that can assist companies in strengthening their connections with their clientele, enhancing their customers' awareness of their brand, and expanding their customer base. Businesses are able to communicate directly with their audience and provide content that is targeted and valuable because they collect email addresses and other contact information from potential customers. This helps build customer loyalty and credibility. Building customer mailing lists is an efficient use of a company's resources, allows for easy expansion, and gives them full command of their marketing activities. As a result, it is an indispensable element of contemporary marketing strategies and a critical factor in the accomplishment of business goals.

Chapter 2: Understanding the Basics of List Building

Building contact lists is an essential part of contemporary marketing strategies, but for those who are just getting started in the field, the process can be quite overwhelming. This chapter will provide an in-depth look at the fundamentals of list building, as well as a step-by-step guide to assist you in getting started.

The first thing you need to do before you start building your list is to determine who your ideal customers are. Who are the individuals that you want to communicate with using your various marketing strategies? What are their areas of interest, the problems they face, and their preferences? You will be able to create content and offers that will resonate with your target audience and encourage them to join your email list if you take the time to understand who they are.

The next step, after determining who your intended audience is, is to develop a lead magnet for potential customers. A lead magnet is a piece of content of significant value that you make available to visitors to your website in exchange for their email addresses. eBooks, whitepapers, checklists, and webinars are all types of content that can serve as lead magnets. Your lead magnet ought to be pertinent to the audience you're trying to reach, and it ought to supply that audience with helpful information that they cannot get anywhere else.

You will need to develop an opt-in form in order to market your lead magnet effectively. A visitor can subscribe to your email list by filling out a form known as an opt-in form when they visit your website. Your website's opt-in form should be displayed in a prominent location, and it should include a call-to-action (CTA) that is both understandable and compelling in order to encourage visitors to sign up.

You may want to consider using pop-ups or other forms of on-site messaging to increase the number of visitors who subscribe to your email list. This can be accomplished by increasing the visibility of the subscription form. However, it is essential to strike a balance between the necessity of promoting your email list and the aspiration of providing a pleasant experience for users. It is important to refrain from using aggressive pop-ups and other intrusive tactics, as these have the potential to irritate and frustrate your site's visitors.

After you have successfully collected email addresses through the use of your opt-in form, the next step is to compose a welcome email. After subscribing to your email list, subscribers' inboxes should immediately be populated with a "welcome" email message. It ought to be friendly and approachable, and it ought to provide subscribers with an outline of the kinds of things they can anticipate seeing in your emails. You might also want to consider including a one-time deal or promotion as an incentive for subscribers to make their initial purchase from your business.

You will need to make sure to send out emails to your subscribers on a consistent basis if you want to maintain their interest in your email list. It is important that the emails you send to your subscribers offer something of value and are pertinent to the interests they have expressed. Depending on the nature of your company and the customers you're trying to attract, you might decide to distribute educational content, promotional emails, or newsletters.

It is important to segment your email list based on the interests of or behaviors exhibited by your subscribers in order to avoid receiving spam complaints or unsubscribe requests. You might, for instance, find it useful to divide customers into two distinct email lists: those who have purchased something from you, and those who have not. You can raise the level of engagement with your subscribers as well as improve the deliverability of your emails if you send them targeted emails.

THE LIST ADVANTAGE: UNLOCKING THE POWER OF LIST BUILDING FOR MARKETING SUCCESS

In conclusion, it is essential to monitor and assess the performance of your email marketing campaigns in order to determine which strategies are successful and which ones are not. The majority of platforms for email marketing provide analytics tools which make it possible to monitor open rates, click-through rates, and other important metrics. You will be able to make educated decisions about how to optimize your email campaigns so that they have the greatest possible impact if you analyze this data first.

In conclusion, the creation of mailing lists is an essential element of contemporary marketing strategies. You can collect email addresses and build a valuable email list if you first determine your target audience, then create a lead magnet, and then promote your email list using opt-in forms and on-site messaging. This will allow you to collect email addresses. It is important to send regular emails that provide value and relevance to your subscribers if you want to maintain their engagement. You can optimize your email marketing campaigns for maximum impact and business success by segmenting your email list and tracking your email marketing campaigns. This will help drive business success.

Chapter 3: The Different Types of Lists and Their Benefits

There is a wide variety of different kinds of lists that companies can use to compile potential clients' contact information and use for marketing purposes. In this chapter, we will discuss the various types of lists that are most commonly used, as well as the benefits associated with them.

1. Email Lists

The most common kind of list that companies use to collect contact information from prospective customers is an email list. An email list is a collection of email addresses that can be used by businesses to send promotional and informative content to their subscribers. Businesses can use email lists to send emails to their email lists.

There are many advantages to using email mailing lists. To begin, they give companies access to the email inboxes of their customers, which enables the companies to communicate directly with the people who are interested in what they have to say. In addition, marketing products and services through email lists is a cost-effective method because companies are able to send targeted messages to individuals who have already indicated an interest in what they have to offer. This makes the use of email lists an extremely useful tool.

In addition, businesses gain a great deal of control over the marketing efforts they undertake thanks to the use of email lists. Businesses have greater say over the content, timing, and frequency of their marketing campaigns when they build and manage their own email lists. This gives them more agency. This provides them with unrestricted authority over their marketing activities and paves the way for them to develop more meaningful connections with their subscribers.

2. Social Media Lists

Individuals who have shown interest in your company or product through the use of social media platforms such as Facebook or Twitter can be compiled into a list and shared across your various social media accounts. These lists can be used to send targeted messages to individuals who have shown interest in your products or services by interacting with your content or by showing that they are engaged with it.

The benefits of using email lists are comparable to the benefits of using social media lists. They make it possible for companies to communicate directly with prospective clients and to send targeted messages to individuals who have indicated an interest in the goods or services being offered by the company. In addition to this, building brand awareness and connecting with new customers can be accomplished at a low cost through the use of social media lists.

3. Lists for Direct Mailing

Direct mail lists are compilations of physical mailing addresses that are made available to companies so that they can send promotional materials to potential customers. Examples of such materials include catalogs and postcards. Direct mail lists can be especially helpful for companies that are aiming their marketing efforts at specific demographics or geographic areas.

Direct mail lists offer a number of advantages to businesses, one of which is the capacity to communicate with prospective clients who might not use the internet or might not have access to an email account. Direct mail can also be a more personalized and tactile way to connect with customers, which enables businesses to create a more memorable experience with their brand.

4. SMS Lists

SMS lists are compilations of phone numbers that companies can use to send text messages to prospective clients. These lists are purchased by the businesses. When it comes to promotions that are time-sensitive or urgent messages, SMS lists can be especially helpful.

THE LIST ADVANTAGE: UNLOCKING THE POWER OF LIST BUILDING FOR MARKETING SUCCESS

The use of short message service (SMS) lists presents businesses with the advantage of being able to communicate with prospective clients who might not use the internet or might not have access to email. In addition, text messages have a high open rate, which makes them an efficient and effective way to communicate with customers in a timely manner.

5. A list of customers

Customer lists are compilations of contact information for individuals who have already made a purchase from your company. These customers have already demonstrated their loyalty to your brand. These lists can be utilized to send specific communications to individuals who have previously indicated an interest in your goods or services.

One of the primary advantages that customer lists offer to businesses is the opportunity to foster brand loyalty and inspire customers to make subsequent purchases. Businesses can build a stronger relationship with their customers and increase the likelihood that those customers will make additional purchases by sending targeted messages to customers who have already made a purchase from the company.

To summarize, businesses have access to a wide variety of list formats to choose from when compiling prospective clients' contact details for use in marketing and sales efforts. Email lists, social media lists, direct mail lists, SMS lists, and customer lists each have their own distinct advantages and can be put to use in a variety of different ways to communicate with prospective customers. Businesses are able to cultivate fruitful relationships with their clientele and increase their chances of commercial success by selecting the appropriate kind of list for their operations.

Chapter 4: Building a High-Quality Email List from Scratch

The development of an email list that is of high quality is an essential component of contemporary marketing strategies. In this chapter, we will discuss the steps that companies can take to construct a high-quality email list from the ground up, beginning with the basics.

First, Determine Who Your Intended Readership Is.

Finding out who you are trying to reach is the first thing you need to do in order to construct an email list of high quality. Who are the individuals that you want to communicate with using your various marketing strategies? What are their areas of interest, the problems they face, and their preferences? You will be able to create content and offers that will resonate with your target audience and encourage them to join your email list if you take the time to understand who they are.

Create a "Lead Magnet" as the Second Step

The next step, after determining who your intended audience is, is to develop a lead magnet for potential customers. A lead magnet is a piece of content of significant value that you make available to visitors to your website in exchange for their email addresses. eBooks, whitepapers, checklists, and webinars are all types of content that can serve as lead magnets. Your lead magnet ought to be pertinent to the audience you're trying to reach, and it ought to supply that audience with helpful information that they cannot get anywhere else.

Create an opt-in form as the third step.

You will need to develop an opt-in form in order to market your lead magnet effectively. A visitor can subscribe to your email list by filling out a form known as an opt-in form when they visit your website. Your website's opt-in form should be displayed in a prominent location, and it should include a call-to-action (CTA) that is both understandable and compelling in order to encourage visitors to sign up.

Your signup form ought to be uncomplicated and straightforward to complete. You should only solicit the data that is absolutely essential to your operation, such as a first name and email address. A visitor's likelihood of filling out your opt-in form decreases proportionately with the number of fields you include in the form.

Step 4: Create a Welcome Email

After you have successfully collected email addresses through the use of your opt-in form, the next step is to compose a welcome email. After subscribing to your email list, subscribers' inboxes should immediately be populated with a "welcome" email message. It ought to be friendly and approachable, and it ought to provide subscribers with an outline of the kinds of things they can anticipate seeing in your emails. You might also want to consider including a one-time deal or promotion as an incentive for subscribers to make their initial purchase from your business.

Step 5: Create Valuable Content In order to maintain the engagement of the people on your email list, you will need to send them regular emails on a consistent basis. It is important that the emails you send to your subscribers offer something of value and are pertinent to the interests they have expressed. Depending on the nature of your company and the customers you're trying to attract, you might decide to distribute educational content, promotional emails, or newsletters.

Your content should be of a high standard and interesting to read. To make your content more appealing, use language that is simple and direct, and incorporate visual elements such as pictures and videos wherever possible. You should give some thought to using a consistent format for your emails, such as a weekly newsletter, to assist in the process of creating familiarity and increasing engagement.

Step 6: Divide Up Your Email List Into Groups

THE LIST ADVANTAGE: UNLOCKING THE POWER OF LIST BUILDING FOR MARKETING SUCCESS

It is important to segment your email list based on the interests of or behaviors exhibited by your subscribers in order to avoid receiving spam complaints or unsubscribe requests. You might, for instance, find it useful to divide customers into two distinct email lists: those who have purchased something from you, and those who have not. You can raise the level of engagement with your subscribers as well as improve the deliverability of your emails if you send them targeted emails.

Step 7: Make Your Email List Known to Others

Last but not least, you should make an effort to promote your email list in order to attract new subscribers. Promoting your lead magnet and encouraging website visitors to sign up for your email list can be accomplished through the use of social media, blog posts, and other marketing channels.

As an incentive for people to sign up for your email list, you might take into consideration providing email subscribers with special deals or discounts. You might also want to think about using pop-ups or other forms of on-site messaging to promote your email list. However, you should be careful to strike a balance between the need to promote your email list and the desire to provide a good user experience.

Chapter 5: Maximizing Your Lead Magnet Strategy for List Building

A lead magnet is a piece of content of significant value that you make available to visitors to your website in exchange for their email addresses. Because it provides an incentive for visitors to subscribe to the owner's email list, it is an indispensable tool for list building. In this chapter, we will discuss how to get the most out of your list-building efforts by making the most of your lead magnet strategy.

1. Identify Your Target Audience

The first thing you need to do in order to make the most of your lead magnet strategy is to determine who your target audience is. Who are the individuals that you want to communicate with using your various marketing strategies? What are their areas of interest, the problems they face, and their preferences? You will be able to create a lead magnet that will resonate with your target audience and encourage people to sign up for your email list if you take the time to understand that audience.

2. Opt for a Subject That Has a Lot of Value

After you have determined who your ideal customers are, the next step is to select a high-value topic for the lead magnet that you will be using. Your lead magnet ought to offer your audience information of significant value, the likes of which they are unable to locate anywhere else. eBooks, whitepapers, checklists, and webinars are all types of content that can serve as lead magnets.

When deciding what to write about in your lead magnet, you should keep in mind the difficulties and annoyances experienced by the people in your target audience. Which information can you give them that will assist them in resolving a problem or accomplishing a goal that they have? Your lead magnet ought to present your audience with insights that are actionable and that they can incorporate into their own lives.

3. Employ a Design of High Quality

It is essential to employ a design of high quality if you want your lead magnet to function at its optimum level of efficiency. Your lead magnet ought to have a pleasant appearance and be straightforward to read. Make your lead magnet stand out from the crowd by using images and graphics of a high quality.

Think about utilizing a recognizable design aesthetic for your lead magnet, such as the colors or fonts associated with your brand. This will help familiarize your audience with your brand and increase the likelihood that they will remember it in the future.

4. Be sure to include a distinct call to action.

Your lead magnet ought to incorporate a distinct call-to-action (CTA) that prompts site visitors to sign up for your email list. Your call to action (CTA) should be displayed in a prominent location on your lead magnet, and it should make the advantages of subscribing to your email list abundantly clear.

Think about using language that highlights the benefits of subscribing to your email list as well as the value of the lead magnet that you are offering. For instance, "Get exclusive access to our weekly newsletter and stay current on the most recent trends in the industry."

5. Get the word out about your lead magnet.

It is important to promote your lead magnet through a variety of marketing channels in order to get the most out of its potential effectiveness. Promote the lead magnet you have created and encourage site visitors to sign up for your email list by posting about it on your blog and other marketing channels, such as social media.

As an incentive for people to sign up for your email list, you might think about offering special deals or discounts that are only available to your email subscribers. You may also want to consider using pop-ups or other forms of on-site messaging to promote your lead magnet.

However, you must ensure that you maintain a healthy balance between the need to promote your lead magnet and the desire to provide a positive user experience.

6. Experiment and Make Adjustments

Last but not least, if you want your lead magnet strategy to be as effective as possible, you need to test it and then optimize it. Utilize A/B testing to conduct experiments with a variety of lead magnet topics, designs, and calls to action (CTAs). Conduct an analysis of the findings of your tests to determine which lead magnets are most successful at attracting new subscribers.

In addition to this, you should monitor how well your lead magnet performs over time. In order to determine whether or not your lead magnet strategy is producing meaningful results for your company, you should examine the quality of your email list as well as the number of sign-ups it has received.

In conclusion, a lead magnet is an indispensable piece of equipment for the process of list building. You can maximize the effectiveness of your lead magnet strategy and build a high-quality email list for your company if you first determine your target audience, then select a high-value topic to write about, use high-quality design, include a clear call-to-action, promote your lead magnet, and test and optimize your strategy.

Chapter 6: Crafting Effective Opt-In Forms and Landing Pages

Opt-in forms and landing pages are two crucial elements that must be included in any list building strategy. These are the instruments that companies employ for the purpose of accumulating email addresses from prospective clients. In this chapter, we will discuss how to effectively craft opt-in forms and landing pages in order to drive conversions.

1. Keep it Simple

The first and most important rule for effectively crafting opt-in forms and landing pages is to keep them as simple as possible. Both the opt-in form and landing page that you use should be straightforward and simple to comprehend. Keep the page as clutter-free as possible and concentrate on the most vital aspects, such as the advantages of subscribing to your email list.

2. Ensure that your headline is both clear and compelling.

When visitors arrive at your opt-in form or landing page, the headline is the very first thing that will appear on their screen. It needs to be understandable as well as compelling, and it needs to convey the advantages of subscribing to your email list. Make use of language that places an emphasis on the worth of your email list as well as the advantages of subscribing to it.

3. Create a Powerful Motivating Factor

It is important to provide a compelling incentive for visitors to your website in order to encourage them to subscribe to your email list. This could take the form of an exclusive piece of content, a limited-time offer, or a lead magnet. Your incentive ought to be pertinent to the audience you're trying to reach and offer them something of genuine value.

4. Reduce the Number of Required Fields on the Form

A visitor's likelihood of filling out an opt-in form decreases proportionately with the number of form fields that are included in the form. Reduce the number of form fields as much as possible and only request the information that is absolutely necessary, such as the user's first name and email address. To achieve a higher rate of conversions, it may be beneficial to use a two-step opt-in process, in which site visitors must first click a button to reveal the opt-in form.

5. Integrate Visuals into Your Site to Improve the User Experience

Your opt-in form or landing page could benefit from the addition of visuals, which could help improve the user experience. You can increase the visual appeal of both your opt-in form and your landing page by using images and graphics of a high quality. Think about directing visitors' attention to the opt-in form with directional indicators like arrows or buttons, for example.

6. Include Evidence from Social Sources

Visitors' perceptions of a website's trustworthiness and credibility can be improved through the use of social proof, such as reviews and testimonials from existing customers. Include social proof on your opt-in form or landing page to reassure visitors that it is worthwhile to subscribe to your email list because it contains valuable information.

7. Ensure You Have a Powerful Call-to-Action

A call-to-action, abbreviated as CTA, refers to the button or link that site visitors are required to click in order to subscribe to an email list. It needs to be understandable as well as compelling, with language that places an emphasis on the advantages of subscribing. Think about using a color that stands out against the background of the page for your call to action (CTA).

8. Experiment and Make Adjustments

In conclusion, it is essential to conduct testing and optimization on both your opt-in form and landing page in order to increase conversions. You can experiment with different headlines, incentives, and calls to action (CTAs) by using A/B testing. Conduct an in-depth

THE LIST ADVANTAGE: UNLOCKING THE POWER OF LIST BUILDING FOR MARKETING SUCCESS

analysis of the results of your testing to establish which aspects are most successful in generating conversions.

In addition to this, you should monitor how well both your opt-in form and landing page perform over time. In order to determine whether or not your opt-in form and landing page are producing meaningful results for your company, you should conduct an analysis of the number of sign-ups as well as the quality of your email list.

To summarize, it is essential to build a high-quality email list by carefully crafting opt-in forms and landing pages that are effective in order to drive conversions. You can make your opt-in forms and landing pages as effective as possible and build a valuable email list for your company if you keep it simple, use a headline that is clear and compelling, offer a strong incentive, keep the number of form fields to a minimum, use visuals to enhance the user experience, include social proof, use a strong call-to-action, and test and optimize your strategy.

Chapter 7: The Anatomy of an Effective Welcome Email

The next step, which takes place after a visitor has subscribed to your email list, is to send that visitor a welcome email. After subscribing to your email list, a new subscriber will initially be greeted with an email known as a welcome email. In this chapter, we will take a look at the components that make up a successful welcome email.

1. A Hearty Greeting to You

A friendly greeting should be included as the first component of an efficient welcome email. Thank the subscriber for signing up for your email list and address them by their first name in the message. Make use of language that is warm and inviting to give the impression that the subscriber is valued and appreciated.

2. An Introduction to Your Company and Your Email List

The following component of a successful welcome email is a summary of your email list as well as your company's brand. Make the most of this opportunity to familiarize the subscriber with your company's brand and to discuss the advantages of signing up for your email list. Give a concise summary of the types of content and deals that subscribers to your email list can anticipate receiving from you in the future.

3. An Invitation to Take Action

Include a call-to-action (CTA) in the email that welcomes new subscribers that encourages them to take some kind of action. This could be a link to your website, an invitation to connect on social media, a unique offer or promotion, or any combination of the three. Your call to action (CTA) needs to be crystal clear and compelling, with language that emphasizes the positive outcomes that result from taking action.

4. A Unique Deal or Advertising Campaign

Consider including a one-time deal or promotion in your welcome message to customers as a way to entice new subscribers to interact with your company and its products. This may come in the form of a coupon code, free shipping, or special access to a piece of content. Your subscriber should receive actual value from the limited-time offer or promotion that you make, and it should be relevant to your brand.

5. Social Proof The use of social proof, such as reviews and testimonials from previous customers, can assist in the development of credibility and trust among subscribers. You can reassure new subscribers that your brand is reliable and valuable by including social proof in the email you send them to welcome them. This may take the form of a review of your products or services, a testimonial from a satisfied customer, or an endorsement from a well-known and respected figure in your field.

6. Links to Relevant Content

You can encourage subscribers to engage with your brand by including links to relevant content in the email you send them when they sign up. This could be a link to a recently published article on the blogger's website, a video tutorial, an eBook, or a white paper. Your links ought to be pertinent to the subscriber's interests and ought to provide real value to the user.

7. Information on How to Get in Touch

Include your contact information in the email that you send to new subscribers as a way to make it simple for them to get in touch with your company. This could be your email address, telephone number, or handles on various social media platforms. Make the most of this chance to encourage subscribers to get in touch with any questions or comments they may have.

8. A note of gratitude

Lastly, you should conclude your welcome email by saying thank you. Express gratitude to new subscribers for signing up for your email list and emphasize how much you appreciate the support they provide.

Make use of language that encourages subscribers to maintain their engagement with your brand and looks forward to further communications by expressing excitement about what's to come.

In conclusion, an efficient welcome email is an essential component of various strategies pertaining to list building. You can create a welcome email that encourages engagement and helps you develop a solid relationship with your subscribers by including a friendly greeting, an overview of your brand and email list, a call to action, a special offer or promotion, social proof, links to content that is relevant to the recipient's interests, contact information, and a thank you message.

Chapter 8: Creating Killer Content to Build Your List

The development of killer content is absolutely necessary in order to construct a robust email list. Your intended readers should perceive that the content you produce has genuine value for them, which will encourage them to sign up for your email newsletter. In this chapter, we will discuss how to create content that is both engaging and effective at growing your email list.

1. Be Familiar with Your Intended Audience

Understanding your intended readers is the first step in the process of developing killer content. Who are the individuals that you want to communicate with using your various marketing strategies? What are their areas of interest, the challenges they face, and their preferences? You will be able to create content that will resonate with your target audience and encourage them to sign up for your email list if you take the time to understand that audience.

2. Pick Subjects That Are Going to Hit Home

After you have determined who your target audience is, the next step is to select topics that will connect with them on a personal level. Your content should provide your audience with valuable information that they cannot find elsewhere. Blog posts, videos, infographics, and podcasts are all types of content that are examples of "killer content."

When selecting a topic for your content, you should take into consideration the problems and obstacles that your target audience is currently dealing with. Which information can you give them that will assist them in resolving a problem or accomplishing a goal that they have? Your content ought to provide insights with a practical application that your audience can put into practice in their own lives.

3. Provide Value

It is essential to provide actual value with your content if you want visitors to subscribe to your email list. This could be information that assists your audience in finding a solution to a problem, advice for achieving a goal, or insights into your industry. Your website's content needs to provide something that readers won't be able to find anywhere else.

4. Make Use of a Powerful Headline

When visitors come across your content, the headline is the very first thing that will come into their view. It needs to be understandable and compelling, and it needs to convey the advantages of reading your content. Make use of language that places an emphasis on the benefits of subscribing to your email list in addition to the value that your content possesses.

5. Employ a Design of High Quality

It is essential to employ design of a high quality if you want your content to be noticeable. Make your content more visually appealing by using photographs and other types of graphics of a high quality. Think about using a design style that is consistent throughout your content, such as the colors or fonts associated with your brand.

6. Be sure to include a direct invitation to take action.

A crystal clear call-to-action (CTA) that encourages visitors to subscribe to your email list should be included in the content that you create. Your call to action (CTA) should be displayed in a prominent location on your content, and it should communicate the advantages of subscribing to your email list very specifically.

7. Promote Your Content

It is imperative that you promote your content through a variety of marketing channels if you wish for it to have the greatest possible impact. You can promote your content and encourage visitors to subscribe to your email list by utilizing social media, email marketing, and any other marketing channels you have access to.

THE LIST ADVANTAGE: UNLOCKING THE POWER OF LIST BUILDING FOR MARKETING SUCCESS

As an incentive for people to sign up for your email list, you might think about offering special deals or discounts that are only available to your email subscribers. You might also want to think about using pop-ups or other types of on-site messaging to promote your content. However, you should strike a balance between the need to promote your content and the desire to provide a good experience for your users.

8. Experiment and Make Adjustments

In conclusion, it is essential to perform testing and optimization on your content in order to get the most out of it. You can experiment with a variety of content topics, headlines, and calls to action (CTAs) by using A/B testing. Conduct an analysis of the results of your testing to determine which types of content are most successful at attracting new subscribers.

In addition to that, you should monitor how well your content performs over time. Determine whether or not your content strategy is producing meaningful results for your company by analyzing the number of sign-ups for your email list as well as the quality of the subscribers on that list.

In conclusion, the production of killer content is an essential component in the development of a robust email list. You can create killer content that builds your email list and drives meaningful results for your business if you know your target audience, choose topics that resonate with them, provide value, use a strong headline, use high-quality design, include a clear call-to-action, promote your content, test and optimize your strategy, and provide value to your readers.

Chapter 9: The Importance of Segmentation and Personalization

Email marketing that is successful must incorporate both email segmentation and personalization in order to be successful. When businesses use segmentation, they are able to divide the subscribers on their email list into targeted groups based on certain criteria. On the other hand, when businesses use personalization, they are able to tailor their messages to each individual subscriber. In the following chapter, we will discuss the significance of email marketing strategies such as personalization and segmentation.

1. An Increase in Its Significance

The relevancy of your email messages can be improved through the use of segmentation and personalization. You can ensure that the content of your email messages is pertinent to the needs and preferences of your audience by segmenting your email list into targeted groups and personalizing the messages you send to each individual subscriber on your list.

2. Improved Engagement

If the messages you send are pertinent to the recipients, they will be more likely to interact with the content you provide. The process of providing subscribers with content that is relevant to their interests and encouraging them to take action is called engagement. Segmentation and personalization are two techniques that can help improve engagement.

3. A Higher Average Rate of Conversion

It is much more likely that subscribers will become paying customers if they are actively engaged with the content that you provide. By providing subscribers with personalized offers and incentives that are pertinent to their interests and preferences, segmentation and personalization can help to increase conversion rates, which is one of the primary goals of digital marketing.

4. Decreases in the Number of Unsubscribe Requests

It is more likely that subscribers will unsubscribe from your email list if they receive messages that are irrelevant to their interests or that do not interest them. By providing subscribers with content that is pertinent to their interests and of value to them, segmentation and personalization can help bring down the rate at which subscribers unsubscribe.

5. Increased Dedication to the Brand

It is more likely that subscribers will feel a sense of loyalty to your brand when they receive personalized messages that provide real value to the recipient. Through the delivery of content that caters to the requirements and pursuits of individual subscribers, segmentation and personalization can assist in the improvement of brand loyalty.

6. An increase in the value of the customer's lifetime

When subscribers feel a sense of loyalty to a company's brand, they are more likely to become repeat customers and to recommend your company to others. By providing subscribers with personalized offers and incentives that encourage them to make repeat purchases, segmentation and personalization can help increase the customer's lifetime value, which in turn increases the value of the customer's business.

7. Improvements Made to the Experience of the Customer

If you send your subscribers personalized messages that are pertinent to them and provide them with value, they are more likely to have a positive experience with your company and its products. By providing subscribers with content that is tailored to their specific requirements and passions, segmentation and personalization can help to improve the overall quality of the customer experience.

8. Increased Accuracy of the Data

THE LIST ADVANTAGE: UNLOCKING THE POWER OF LIST BUILDING FOR MARKETING SUCCESS

You can ensure that the data you use is correct and up to date by segmenting your email list based on specific criteria. Because of this, you will have access to more accurate data on the actions and preferences of your subscribers, which can help improve the efficiency of your email marketing campaigns.

9. Improved Capabilities in the Areas of Testing and Optimization

You will be able to test and improve the performance of your email marketing campaigns more effectively if you segment your email list and personalize your messages. You can determine which strategies are most effective at driving engagement and conversions by analyzing the performance of various segments and messages in order to find out which ones perform the best.

In conclusion, the most successful email marketing strategies incorporate both segmentation and personalization into their strategies. Segmentation and personalization can help businesses build stronger relationships with their subscribers and drive meaningful results for their businesses. These benefits can be achieved by increasing relevance, improving engagement, increasing conversion rates, reducing unsubscribe rates, improving brand loyalty, increasing customer lifetime value, enhancing the customer experience, improving data accuracy, and enabling more effective testing and optimization.

Chapter 10: Developing a Winning Email Marketing Strategy

List building, content creation, audience segmentation, and personalization are the four components that must be thoughtfully combined in order to develop a successful strategy for email marketing. In this chapter, we will discuss the essential components of a successful email marketing strategy, as well as the steps necessary to create such a strategy for your company.

1. Lay Out Your Objectives

The first thing you need to do in order to create a successful strategy for email marketing is to define your goals. What are you hoping to accomplish with the efforts you put into email marketing? Increasing sales, driving traffic to a website, increasing brand awareness, and promoting new products or services are some examples of goals that can be accomplished through email marketing.

2. Compile a list of your email addresses.

Creating an email list is the next thing you should do. To increase the number of people who sign up for your email list, you can employ a number of different list building strategies, such as landing pages, opt-in forms, and lead magnets. As an incentive for people to sign up for your email list, you might take into consideration providing email subscribers with special deals or discounts.

3. Come up with Content That Kills

It is important to create killer content that provides real value to your subscribers in order to maintain their engagement. Make sure to use a design that is of high quality and incorporate distinct calls to action (CTAs) that will encourage subscribers to take action.

4. Segment Your Email List

You can provide targeted messages that are relevant to each subscriber by segmenting your email list based on specific criteria, such as demographics, behavior, and interests. For example, you could use these categories. You can improve engagement with your subscribers by using personalization to tailor your messages to each individual subscriber.

5. Determine the frequency of your outgoing messages.

Determine how frequently you will send out emails to your subscribers and stick to that schedule. This will be determined by the goals you have set for yourself as well as the preferences of your subscribers. Consider running experiments with a variety of sending frequencies to identify the one that encourages the most effective levels of engagement and conversions.

6. Experiment and Make Adjustments

You can improve the effectiveness of your email marketing campaigns by testing and optimizing them. You can use A/B testing to experiment with a variety of content topics, headlines, and calls to action. Conduct an in-depth analysis of the results of your tests to establish which strategies are most successful in generating user engagement and conversions.

7. Measure Your Results

You can determine the efficiency of your email marketing campaigns by measuring the results of those campaigns. To determine the efficacy of your email marketing efforts, you should conduct an analysis of various metrics, including open rates, click-through rates, conversion rates, and unsubscribe rates.

8. Make sure that you are always working to improve your strategy.

Your strategy for marketing via email should always be refined based on the results you get. You can improve your content, segmentation, and personalization, as well as your sending frequency, by using the data you collect. If you want to grow your email list and attract new subscribers, you should think about testing new list building strategies.

9. Ensure That You Are Always In Compliance With Regulations

THE LIST ADVANTAGE: UNLOCKING THE POWER OF LIST BUILDING FOR MARKETING SUCCESS

Make sure that the laws that govern email marketing, such as the CAN-SPAM Act, are followed by your business when conducting email marketing. This includes providing a distinct opt-out option in each and every email and including the physical address of your company in each and every email.

In conclusion, developing a successful strategy for email marketing necessitates using a combination of list building, content creation, segmentation, and personalization in a thoughtful and deliberate manner. You can develop an email marketing strategy for your company that generates engagement, conversions, and results that are meaningful by first determining your goals, then building your email list, then developing killer content, then segmenting your email list, then determining your sending frequency, then testing and optimizing, then measuring your results, then continuously improving your strategy, and finally maintaining compliance with regulations.

Chapter 11: Mastering the Art of Email Copywriting

Email copywriting that is effective is absolutely necessary if you want your email marketing campaigns to generate meaningful results, levels of engagement, and conversions. In this chapter, we will delve into the fundamentals of compelling email copywriting and discuss how to become an expert in the art of penning persuasive electronic correspondence.

1. Be Aware of Your Target Market

Understanding your target market is the first step in writing compelling copy for emails. Who are the individuals that you want to communicate with using your various marketing strategies? What are their areas of interest, the problems they face, and their preferences? You will be able to write copy that resonates with your audience and encourages them to take action if you take the time to learn about them.

2. Compose a Subject Line That Is Powerful

When subscribers open your email, the subject line that you choose to include will be the first thing that they see. It needs to be understandable and compelling, and it needs to convey the advantages of reading your email. Make sure to use language that places an emphasis on the significance of your email as well as the advantages of responding.

3. Ensure That Your Headline Is Both Clear And Enticing

Your email's headline ought to be easy to understand and compelling, offering a synopsis of the benefits that can be gained from reading your email. Make use of language that immediately captures the attention of the reader and inspires them to keep reading.

4. Get Right to the Point in a Hurry

When crafting the body of an email, it is critical to cut to the chase and get to the point as soon as possible. Subscribers are typically very busy people who have short attention spans. Make sure to communicate the value of your email in a clear and concise manner that motivates your subscribers to take some sort of action.

5. Use Persuasive Language

When writing the copy for your email, use language that is convincing to encourage readers to take some sort of action. Make use of words and phrases that call attention to the many advantages of your offer and instill a sense of immediacy. Think about using social proof, such as reviews or testimonials from previous customers, to build subscribers' trust in you and your business's credibility.

6. Be sure to include a direct invitation to take action.

A crystal clear call-to-action (CTA) that encourages subscribers to take action should be included in the email you send them. Your call to action (CTA) should be displayed prominently and communicate the benefits of acting in a clear and concise manner.

7. Employ a Design of High Quality

It is essential to make use of a design of high quality if you want your email to be noticed. Make your email more visually appealing by incorporating high-quality images and graphics into it. Think about using a design style that is consistent throughout your email, such as the colors or fonts associated with your brand.

8. Maintain Coherence in the Voice of Your Brand

Your brand voice ought to be used consistently throughout the copy of your emails. Make sure that the language and tone you use reflect the personality and ideals of your brand. This will help build trust and credibility with your subscribers, and it will also help create a stronger connection between your brand and your audience.

9. Use Personalization

Through the customization of your messages to each individual subscriber, personalization can assist in increasing engagement and conversion rates. Make use of subscriber data, such as a person's name, location, or purchase history, to customize the content of your email messages and provide subscribers with a more individualized experience.

10. Check for errors and make edits

Be sure to proofread and edit your copy before sending your email and correct any errors you may find. Make sure that your writing is error-free in terms of spelling and grammar, and that it is also crystal clear, succinct, and compelling. You should think about testing out several different versions of the copy in your emails to see which one is most successful at generating engagement and conversions.

In conclusion, mastering the art of email copywriting calls for a combination of thinking strategically, using language that is persuasive, and designing in a high-quality way. You are able to produce email copy that generates engagement, conversions, and meaningful results for your company if you are familiar with your target audience, if you write an effective subject line and headline, if you get to the point quickly, if you use persuasive language and social proof if you include a clear call-to-action if you use high-quality design if you are consistent with your brand voice if you utilize personalization and if you proofread and edit your work.

Chapter 12: A/B Testing Your Emails for Optimal Results

Testing with the A/B method is a powerful tool that can be used to improve the efficiency of your email marketing campaigns. You can determine which strategies are most effective at driving engagement and conversions by testing different variations of your emails and analyzing the results of those tests. In this chapter, we will discuss the fundamentals of A/B testing and how to apply the methodology to improve the performance of your email marketing campaigns.

1. Lay Out Your Objectives

Establishing your goals is the initial step in conducting A/B testing on your emails. What are you hoping to accomplish with the efforts you put into email marketing? Increasing open rates, click-through rates, conversion rates, and revenue are some examples of goals that can be attained through email marketing.

2. Choose Your Variables

Choose the different aspects of your email marketing campaigns that you would like to put to the test. Message subject lines, headlines, content topics, calls to action (CTAs), and sending frequency are all examples of variables. Choose the variables that have the greatest potential to have an effect on the success of your email marketing campaigns.

3. Determine Your Sample Size

Find out how many people will be in your sample population. The larger the number of people in your sample, the more reliable your findings will be. You should give some thought to using statistical analysis to figure out how large of a sample you need for your A/B testing.

4. Make Your Own Unique Variations

Create at least two and possibly more variants of your email, each of which should contain a different variable for you to test. You could, for instance, create two versions of your email with two different subject lines or two versions of your email with two different calls to action. Make certain that each variation is unique, and that the variable that is being tested is the only factor that differentiates the different versions.

5. Ensure You Send Out Your Emails

Send your emails to your sample population. In order to ensure that the results are reliable, it is imperative that each version be distributed to an equivalent number of subscribers.

6. Carry out an analysis of your results.

Conduct an analysis of the results of your A/B tests to determine which variation performs best in terms of generating engagement and conversions. To determine which version is the most successful, it is necessary to conduct an analysis of various metrics, including open rates, click-through rates, conversion rates, and revenue.

7. Put your findings into action.

You can improve the effectiveness of your email marketing campaigns by putting the findings from your A/B testing into action. Utilize the findings to improve your email marketing strategy by, for example, adopting the subject line or call to action (CTA) that performed the best in your A/B testing.

8. Carry out ongoing testing and improvements.

A/B testing should be used to continuously improve and optimize the performance of your email marketing campaigns. You can determine which strategies are most effective at driving engagement and conversions by conducting experiments with a variety of variables and analyzing the results of those experiments. Make use of the findings to improve the effectiveness of your email marketing strategy and ensure that it remains up to date.

In conclusion, A/B testing is an effective method for improving the efficiency of your email marketing campaigns using a powerful tool known as split testing. You can use A/B testing to drive engagement, conversions, and meaningful results for your business if you first define your goals, then choose your variables, then determine your sample size, then create your variations, send your emails, analyze your results, implement your findings, and continuously test and optimize.

Chapter 13: Automating Your List Building and Email Marketing

Your efforts to streamline your list building and email marketing can be greatly assisted by automation, which is a powerful tool. You can improve the efficiency of your email marketing campaigns while simultaneously saving time by automating key processes. These processes include the delivery of lead magnets and welcome email campaigns. In this chapter, we will discuss the fundamentals of list building and email marketing automation, as well as the steps necessary to put these strategies into action for your company.

1. Lay Out Your Objectives

Specifying your objectives is the first thing you need to do before beginning to automate the process of list building and email marketing. What are you hoping to accomplish with the efforts you put into email marketing? Increasing sales, driving traffic to a website, increasing brand awareness, and promoting new products or services are some examples of goals that can be accomplished through email marketing.

2. Select the Platform You Will Use for Automation

Select an automation platform that can cater to the requirements of your company. Mailchimp, HubSpot, and ConvertKit are three well-known examples of popular automation platforms. Think about things like how simple the software is to use, how much it costs, and which features are the most essential for your company.

3. Establish an automated system for list building

You can improve the efficiency of your lead generation efforts by automating the process of list building. You can entice people to visit your website and persuade them to subscribe to your email list by providing them with lead magnets, opt-in forms, and landing pages. Make use of automation tools to send lead magnets to your subscribers and to follow up with them. This will encourage engagement.

4. Implement Welcome Email Automation

Greeting new subscribers with a warm and friendly email is a great way to make a good first impression on them. Make use of automation to send a welcome email series to new subscribers. This series should introduce new subscribers to your brand and encourage them to become engaged. Include details about your company, any current promotions, and links to your website and social media channels, as well as any other relevant information.

5. Put in place an automated triggered email system.

Employ automated email sending that is triggered in response to specific subscriber actions in order to send targeted communications to subscribers. Emails sent in response to events such as an abandoned shopping cart, post-purchase follow-ups, or re-engagement are all examples of triggered emails. Make use of automation to send these messages at the appropriate time to subscribers, and encourage them to take some sort of action.

6. Implement Drip Campaign Automation

Automating the delivery of a series of targeted messages to subscribers over the course of a drip campaign is a useful strategy. Make use of automation so that these messages can be scheduled based on the actions and preferences of subscribers. The cultivation of leads, promotion of products or services, and the encouragement of engagement are all possible uses for drip marketing campaigns.

7. Put your automation through its paces and work to improve it.

You can improve the efficiency of your automation by testing it and optimizing it. Experiment with a variety of email messages and automation sequences by using A/B testing. Conduct a thorough analysis of the data to establish which strategies are the most successful in generating engagement and conversions.

8. Make consistent efforts to enhance your automation

Your results should serve as the basis for ongoing improvements to your automation. Make use of the information you collect to improve the automation of your drip campaign by refining your list building, welcome email, triggered email, and other email campaigns. If you want to improve your results, you should think about testing out new automation sequences or email messages.

In conclusion, automation is a powerful tool that can streamline your efforts to build your email list and market your business online. You can use automation to drive engagement, conversions, and meaningful results for your business if you first define your goals, then select your automation platform, then implement list building automation, welcome email automation, triggered email automation, and drip campaign automation, test and optimize your automation, and continuously improve your automation.

Chapter 14: The Role of Social Media in List Building

The use of social media, which is a powerful tool for list building, can assist you in expanding your email list as well as reaching new audiences. In this chapter, we will discuss the most important aspects of using social media for list building, as well as the most effective ways to leverage social media in order to grow your email subscriber base.

1. Determine Which Social Media Platforms You Will Use

Select the social media platforms that will provide the greatest value to both your company and your audience. Facebook, Instagram, Twitter, LinkedIn, and Pinterest are some examples of popular social media platforms. Other examples include Google+ and YouTube. When deciding which social media platforms to use, you should take into account the demographics and interests of your intended audience.

2. Create a Social Media Strategy

Develop a social media strategy that is in line with the objectives you have set for list building. Make use of social media to spread the word about your lead magnets, opt-in forms, and landing pages, and encourage your followers to join your email list. You should think about using ads on social media to target specific audiences and promote your efforts to build a mailing list.

3. To build your brand, make use of social media.

Make use of social media to strengthen your online presence and build your brand's reputation. Make your social media profiles more visually appealing and in line with your brand identity by using high-quality images and graphics. Maintaining a consistent presence on social media and interacting with your audience can help you gain credibility and trust.

4. Promote Your Lead Magnets

To grow your email list with new subscribers, you should promote the lead magnets you have created on social media. To entice followers to click through to your landing pages and opt-in forms, you can employ graphics that are appealing to the eye and language that is convincing. As an incentive for people to sign up for your service, you might think about offering followers of your social media accounts special discounts or promotions.

5. Use Social Media Ads

You can target specific audiences with social media ads and promote your efforts to build a mailing list by doing so. You can reach audiences based on their demographics, interests, and behaviors by making use of the targeting options that are available on social media platforms. Consider running experiments with a variety of different ad formats, such as carousel ads or video ads, to determine which ones are most successful at generating user engagement and sales.

6. Interact with Those Who Follow You

Build relationships with the people who follow you on social media and encourage them to engage by talking to them. Quickly respond to people's comments and messages, and provide information and resources that are helpful. Encourage your followers to sign up for your email list and to share your content with the networks that they are a part of.

7. Make Use of the Social Proof

You can build your social media followers' trust and credibility by providing them with social proof, such as reviews or testimonials from previous customers. Share the positive feedback that you've received from pleased customers, and ask your followers to leave you reviews or testimonials on your various social media profiles.

8. Measure Your Results

You can determine the efficiency of your efforts to build your social media list by measuring the results of those efforts. You can determine the impact of your social media marketing efforts by conducting an analysis of metrics such as engagement rates, click-through rates, conversion rates, and the growth of your follower base.

In conclusion, social media platforms are an effective tool for list building that can assist you in expanding your email list as well as reaching new audiences. You can effectively leverage social media to grow your email list and drive meaningful results for your business if you choose your social media platforms carefully, develop a social media strategy, use social media to build your brand, promote your lead magnets, make use of social media ads, engage with your followers, make use of social proof, and measure your results.

Chapter 15: Using Influencer Marketing to Build Your List

Building up your email list and expanding your reach can both be accomplished effectively through the use of influencer marketing. You can promote your brand and encourage followers to subscribe to your email list by partnering with influencers who have a large number of followers who are actively involved in the activity. In this chapter, we will discuss the fundamentals of utilizing influencer marketing for the purpose of list building, as well as the most effective ways to leverage influencers in order to expand your email subscriber base.

1. Lay Out Your Objectives

Determining your objectives comes first in the process of using influencer marketing to build your email list. What are you hoping to accomplish with the efforts you put into your influencer marketing? Increasing the number of people who sign up for email lists, boosting traffic to a website, and cultivating brand awareness are all examples of goals.

2. Pick Your Most Important Influencers

Choose to collaborate with influential people who have a sizable and active following that is in line with your ideal customers. Think about things like the influencer's audience demographics and engagement rates as well as the niche that they serve. Keep an eye out for influential people who have a proven track record of promoting brands and producing results that are meaningful.

3. Work on Creating Your Offer

Create an incentive for influencers to promote your brand and encourage their followers to sign up for your email list by creating an offer that they can take advantage of. Some examples of offers include early access to unreleased products or services, early access to exclusive discounts or promotions, early access to premium content, and so on.

4. Establish Your Marketing Strategy

Create a campaign that will promote your brand and encourage followers to sign up for your email list by effectively leveraging the influence of key opinion leaders in your industry. When developing your campaign, you should take into account the influencer's platform and audience, and you should tailor your messaging to the specific needs of their audience.

5. Track Your Results

Keep an eye on the results of your influencer marketing campaign so you can evaluate how successful it was. You can determine the effectiveness of your campaign by conducting an analysis of various metrics, including the number of people who sign up for your email list, the amount of traffic to your website, and the amount of engagement on social media. Make use of these data to improve the effectiveness of your influencer marketing strategy and to ensure that it continues to evolve.

6. Engage in Further Communication with New Subscribers

Maintain communication with any new subscribers who became part of your audience as a direct result of your influencer marketing campaign. Introduce new subscribers to your brand and encourage them to engage with it through the use of a welcome email series. Consider offering exclusive promotions or discounts to incentivize engagement.

7. Keep your relationships with those who have influence.

Maintain relationships with influencers to build trust and credibility. Maintain consistent communication with them and add value by providing them with useful information and a variety of resources. Consider partnering with influencers on future campaigns to continue to drive meaningful results.

8. Make steady progress in the development of your influencer marketing strategy

Your strategy for marketing through influencers should be continuously improved based on the results. Use the data you collect to refine your targeting, messaging, and offer. Think about conducting experiments with new platforms or influencers to find out which ones are the most successful at generating engagement and conversions.

In conclusion, influencer marketing is a powerful tool for building your email list and reaching new audiences. By defining your goals, choosing your influencers, developing your offer, developing your campaign, tracking your results, following up with new subscribers, maintaining relationships with influencers, and continuously improving your influencer marketing strategy, you can effectively leverage influencer marketing to grow your email list and drive meaningful results for your business.

Chapter 16: Harnessing the Power of Referral Marketing

Marketing through word of mouth is an effective method for expanding your email subscriber base and producing results that are meaningful for your company. You can leverage the power of word-of-mouth marketing to grow your email list and drive conversions if you encourage happy customers to refer their friends and family members to your brand. In this chapter, we will discuss the most important aspects of utilizing referral marketing for the purpose of list building, as well as the most effective ways to harness the power of referrals to grow your email list.

1. Define Your Goals

Establishing your goals is the first thing you need to do before beginning to build your email list with referral marketing. What are you hoping to accomplish with the efforts you put into marketing through referrals? Increasing the number of people who sign up for email lists, boosting traffic to a website, and cultivating brand awareness are all examples of goals.

2. Establish a program for receiving referrals

Create a referral program that offers satisfied customers an incentive to recommend your company's products and services to their friends and family members. Incentives can take many forms, such as special discounts or promotions, free goods or services, or early access to newly released goods or services.

3. Make sure to publicize your referral program.

It is important to promote your referral program in order to encourage happy customers to recommend your product or service to their friends and family. Promote your referral program and encourage people to sign up for it through the use of email marketing, social media, and your website.

4. Keep Tabs on Your Outcomes

Maintain a record of the outcomes of your referral marketing program so that you can evaluate its efficiency. To determine the impact of your program, conduct an analysis of various metrics, including the number of people who sign up for your email list, the amount of traffic to your website, and the conversion rate for referrals. Make use of this data to improve your referral marketing strategy, which will in turn help you achieve ever-better results.

5. Engage in Further Communication with New Subscribers

Maintain communication with new subscribers who have joined as a direct result of your referral marketing program. Introduce new subscribers to your brand and encourage them to engage with it through the use of a welcome email series. To encourage people to participate in your campaign, you might think about providing them with access to special discounts or promotions.

6. Keep up your relationships with people who send you referrals

Building trust and credibility requires maintaining relationships with those who can provide referrals. Maintain consistent communication with them and add value by providing them with useful information and a variety of resources. Consider rewarding or incentivizing referrers who consistently drive meaningful results for your company by providing them with perks such as discounts or free products.

7. Make Constant Efforts to Enhance Your Strategy for Referral Marketing

Your strategy for marketing through referrals should constantly be improved based on the results. Make use of the information you collect to hone your approach to targeting, as well as your messaging and offer. You might want to run experiments with different incentive or referral program structures to find out which ones are the most successful at driving engagement and conversions.

In conclusion, referral marketing is an effective tool that can help you build your email list and generate meaningful results for your company. You will be able to effectively harness the power of referrals to grow your email list and drive meaningful results for your company if you first define your goals, then develop your referral program, then promote your referral program, track your results, follow up with new subscribers, maintain relationships with referrers, and continuously improve your referral marketing strategy.

Chapter 17: Creating a Sense of Urgency to Encourage Sign-Ups

Developing a sense of imminence can be an efficient strategy for increasing the number of people who sign up for newsletters and driving conversions. You can motivate potential subscribers to take action and sign up for your email list if you frame your offer in a way that suggests there is a limited supply of something or that there is a time limit on it. In this chapter, we will discuss the essential components of developing a sense of urgency in order to encourage sign-ups, as well as the most effective ways to utilize urgency in order to expand the size of your email list.

1. Define Your Goals

Establishing your goals is the first thing you need to do in order to generate a feeling of imminence and encourage people to sign up. What are you hoping to accomplish with your email campaigns that emphasize the sense of urgency? Increasing the number of people who sign up for email lists, boosting traffic to a website, and cultivating brand awareness are all examples of goals.

2. Create an offer that is based on the sense of urgency.

Create a limited-time offer with a sense of urgency in order to encourage prospective subscribers to take action and sign up for your email list. Promotions that are only available for a limited amount of time, exclusive discounts or deals, and free gifts or bonuses for subscribers who sign up by a certain date are all examples of offers that are based on the concept of urgency.

3. Create Messaging That Is Compelling

Develop persuasive messaging that places an emphasis on the time sensitivity and value of your offer. Create a sense of excitement and urgency about your offer by employing language that is convincing and graphics that grab the attention of the reader. Bring attention to the advantages of subscribing to your email list as well as the benefits that subscribers will derive from the content you provide them.

4. Make Use of Calls to Action That Are Based on Urgency

You can encourage potential subscribers to take action and sign up for your email list by using calls to action that emphasize the sense of urgency. Make use of phrases like "Limited time only" and "Act now before it's too late" to emphasize the time-sensitive nature and sense of urgency associated with your offer. To put even more stress on the immediacy of your offer, you might want to think about incorporating visual elements such as countdown timers.

5. Segment Your Audience

You can target specific groups of potential subscribers with time-sensitive offers that are crafted to meet their specific interests and requirements if you segment your audience first. Targeting subscribers who are most likely to be interested in your offer can be accomplished with the help of data such as previous purchasing behavior or activity on your website.

6. Put Your Campaigns to the Test and Keep Improving Them

Your email campaigns that are based on the sense of urgency should be tested and improved in order to determine which types of messaging and offers are most successful at generating sign-ups and conversions. You can determine which aspects of your campaigns, such as subject lines, messaging, and offers, are most successful at generating engagement and conversions by using A/B testing to compare and contrast the two versions of those aspects.

7. Engage in Further Communication with New Subscribers

Maintain communication with new subscribers who have joined your list as a direct result of your email campaigns that emphasize the sense of urgency. Introduce new subscribers to your brand and encourage them to engage with it through the use of a welcome email series. As an incentive for participation, you might think about providing access to special sales or discounts.

8. Make Constant Efforts to Enhance the Urgency of Your Email Marketing Campaigns

Always work to improve the effectiveness of your time-sensitive email marketing campaigns based on the data you collect. Make use of the information you collect to hone your approach to targeting, as well as your messaging and offer. You should think about conducting experiments to determine which new urgency-based offers or messaging are most successful at attracting signups and converting visitors into customers.

To summarize, cultivating a sense of imminence can be an efficient way to increase the number of people who sign up for your newsletter and drive conversions. You can effectively leverage urgency to grow your email list and drive meaningful results for your business if you first define your goals, then develop your urgency-based offer, then craft compelling messaging, then use urgency-based calls to action; then segment your audience; test and refine your campaigns; follow up with new subscribers; and continuously improve your urgency-based email campaigns.

Chapter 18: The Benefits of Offering Lead Magnets and Freebies

A powerful tactic for growing your email list and increasing conversions is to make lead magnets and other freebies available to your audience. You can entice people who might be interested in subscribing to your email list and build trust and credibility with your audience if you provide useful content or resources in exchange for their email addresses. In this chapter, we will discuss the primary advantages of providing lead magnets and freebies, as well as the most effective ways to make use of this strategy in order to expand the size of your email list.

1. Bring in a Greater Number of Registered Users

The provision of lead magnets and freebies is a potent method for attracting more individuals to sign up for one's email list. You can encourage people who might be interested in subscribing to take action and sign up for your email list by giving them something of value in exchange for their email address.

2. Establish Your Credibility and Gain People's Trust

Building your audience's trust and establishing your credibility can be facilitated tremendously by providing them with freebies and lead magnets of a high standard. You can demonstrate both your expertise and your dedication to providing value to your audience by giving away something of value to them at no cost.

3. Segment Your Audience

Your audience can be segmented so that you can target specific groups of potential subscribers with content that is tailored to their interests and needs if you offer lead magnets and freebies. This can help you increase the number of subscribers you have. You can effectively target and engage with different groups of potential subscribers if you tailor the lead magnets and freebies that you provide for the various subsets of your audience.

4. Drive both engagement and conversions with your content.

Increasing engagement and conversions can also be accomplished by providing lead magnets and freebies. You can encourage potential subscribers to engage with your brand and take action, such as making a purchase or signing up for a paid subscription, by providing something of value to them for free and making it available to them.

5. Provide Value to Your Audience

Providing freebies and lead magnets of high quality to your audience is another fantastic way to add value to what you have to offer. By demonstrating your dedication to providing value to your audience and cultivating relationships with them, offering something of value to them at no cost demonstrates that commitment.

6. Illustrate the Depth of Your Knowledge

You can demonstrate your expertise and establish yourself as an authority in your field by providing lead magnets and freebies to the people who sign up for your email list. You can demonstrate your knowledge and expertise to your audience, as well as build trust and credibility with them, if the content or resources you provide are of a high quality and are tailored to meet the needs of your audience.

7. Raise Consumer Awareness of the Product

Increasing brand awareness can also be accomplished by providing lead magnets and freebies to potential customers. You can bring in new potential subscribers and introduce them to your brand by giving away something of value to them for free. These prospective subscribers become more familiar with your brand as they engage with your content and resources, which increases the likelihood that they will become customers or advocates of your business.

8. Make room for cross-selling and upselling opportunities

Creating opportunities for upselling is another benefit that can come from offering lead magnets and freebies. You can introduce potential customers to your brand and build relationships with them by giving away content or resources that are related to the products or services that you sell for a fee. It is possible that the likelihood of these prospective customers making a purchase or upgrading to a paid subscription will increase as they engage more with your brand and become more acquainted with the products or services you offer.

In conclusion, providing lead magnets and freebies is an effective strategy for building your email list and driving conversions. This can be accomplished by offering a combination of the two. You can effectively leverage this strategy to grow your email list and drive meaningful results for your business by attracting more subscribers, establishing trust and credibility, segmenting your audience, driving engagement and conversions, providing value to your audience, showcasing your expertise, increasing brand awareness, and creating opportunities for upselling.

Chapter 19: How to Measure the Success of Your List Building Efforts

It is essential to measure the success of your efforts to build your email list in order to understand how effective your email marketing strategy is and to identify areas in which you can make improvements. You can gain valuable insights into the performance of your email campaigns and make decisions that are data-driven to improve your results if you track key metrics and analyze data. In this chapter, we will go over the most important metrics to keep track of as well as discuss how to effectively measure the success of your efforts to build a list.

1. The Rate of New Email Subscribers

The percentage of people who visit your website and then sign up for your email list is referred to as the email sign-up rate. This metric is an important indicator of how successful your opt-in forms, landing pages, and lead magnets are in attracting new subscribers. Your opt-in forms and landing pages must be doing a good job of convincing visitors to sign up for your email list if you have a high sign-up rate for your emails.

2. The Rate of Conversion

The conversion rate is the percentage of email subscribers who take an action that is desired, such as making a purchase or signing up for a paid subscription. This could include signing up for a paid newsletter. This metric is an important indicator of how successful your email marketing campaigns have been in generating conversions and revenue so far. Your ability to effectively motivate subscribers to take action can be measured by the conversion rate of your email marketing campaigns.

3. Open Rate

The percentage of subscribers who actually open your email campaigns is referred to as the open rate. This metric is an important indicator of how effective your subject lines are, as well as how your sender reputation is perceived. A high open rate shows that your subject lines are successfully enticing subscribers to open your emails, and it also indicates that your sender reputation is strong.

4. Percentage of Users Who Click

The percentage of subscribers who actually take action and click on a link within your email campaign is referred to as the click-through rate. This metric is an important indicator of how effective the content of your emails and the calls to action within them are. A high click-through rate demonstrates that the content of your emails is successfully capturing the attention of your subscribers and that your calls to action are successfully inspiring them to take the desired action.

5. Rate of Unsubscription

The percentage of subscribers who decide to remove themselves from your email list is known as the unsubscribe rate. This metric is an important indicator of how well your email campaigns are living up to the expectations of your subscribers, and it can be found in the table below. If your unsubscribe rate is high, it may be an indication that the content of your emails is not living up to the requirements or requirements of your subscribers.

6. The rate of bounces

The percentage of email campaigns that are sent out and then bounced back to the sender as a result of invalid email addresses or other delivery problems is referred to as the bounce rate. This metric is an important indicator of the quality of your email list as well as the efficiency of the email verification processes that you have in place. If your email list has a high bounce rate, it may be because it contains email addresses that are no longer valid or are out of date.

7. Return on Investment (ROI) Return on investment (ROI) is a measure of the financial return on your efforts to market your business via email. This metric is an essential indicator of how successful your email marketing campaigns are in terms of generating revenue and moving your company closer to achieving its objectives. When your

THE LIST ADVANTAGE: UNLOCKING THE POWER OF LIST BUILDING FOR MARKETING SUCCESS

return on investment (ROI) is high, it shows that the email marketing strategy you are using is successfully driving revenue and making a positive contribution to the success of your company.

It is important to keep track of these key metrics over time and use them to identify areas that need improvement if you want to effectively measure the success of your efforts to build your list. You can determine which aspects of your email marketing campaigns, such as subject lines, messaging, and calls to action, are most successful at generating engagement and conversions by using A/B testing. Conduct data analysis to spot recurring themes and tendencies, then make use of the insights gained from this exercise to refine and perfect your email marketing approach.

In conclusion, it is essential to measure the success of your list building efforts in order to gain an understanding of the effectiveness of your email marketing strategy and to locate areas in which improvements can be made. You can gain valuable insights into the performance of your email campaigns and make decisions that are data-driven to improve your results if you track key metrics such as the rate at which people sign up for your email list, the conversion rate, the open rate, the click-through rate, the rate at which people unsubscribe, and the bounce rate.

Chapter 20: Staying Compliant with Email Marketing Regulations

The regulations governing email marketing are meant to protect customers and guarantee that businesses will adhere to moral and open-minded business practices when sending marketing emails. If you do not comply with these regulations, you may face legal repercussions, suffer damage to your reputation, and see a reduction in the amount of trust your audience has in you. In this chapter, we will discuss the most important regulations that pertain to email marketing, as well as the best practices for maintaining compliance.

1. The CAN-SPAM Act

The CAN-SPAM Act is a federal law that was passed in the United States in 2003 and is responsible for establishing guidelines for commercial email communications. In order to comply with the CAN-SPAM Act, businesses are required to: • Include an opt-out mechanism that is both clear and prominent in all marketing emails

• Always include an accurate and non-misleading subject line in marketing emails • Always identify marketing emails as advertisements • Always provide a valid physical postal address in marketing emails • Always include an accurate and non-misleading subject line in marketing emails • Always include an accurate and non-misleading subject line in marketing emails

2. GDPR

The General Data Protection Regulation, also known as GDPR, is a regulation that was enacted by the European Union (EU) in order to establish standards for the safeguarding of personal information and the protection of an individual's right to privacy. In order to comply with the General Data Protection Regulation (GDPR), businesses are required to: • Obtain the individuals' clear consent before collecting or processing their personal data; • Give individuals the ability to access, correct, and delete their personal data; • Take precautions to protect personal data from unauthorized access, loss, or theft; and • Notify individuals in the event of a data breach.

3. Canadian Anti-Spam Legislation (CASL) The Canadian Anti-Spam Legislation (CASL) is a piece of legislation that establishes guidelines for the transmission of commercial electronic messages in Canada. In order to comply with CASL, businesses are required to:
• Obtain consent from individuals, either express or implied, before sending them commercial electronic messages

• Include accurate identification information in all marketing emails • Include a mechanism that makes it obvious and easy to opt out of receiving emails from the company • Ensure that any opt-out mechanism is clear and prominent

4. The Most Effective Methods for Maintaining Compliance

In addition to adhering to certain regulations, staying in compliance with regulations governing email marketing requires following a number of best practices, which are as follows:

• Obtain subscribers' explicit consent before adding them to your email list; • Provide subscribers with information that is both clear and concise about your email marketing practices and how their personal data will be used; • Honor unsubscribe requests promptly and without exception; • Use subject lines that are accurate and non-deceptive and that clearly describe the content of your email; • Avoid using language that is misleading or spammy in your emails; • Regularly clean and update your email list

It is important to regularly review and update your email marketing practices in order to maintain compliance with the regulations governing email marketing. This will ensure that you are not in violation of these regulations. Think about carrying out a compliance audit in order to evaluate the procedures you currently use and find places where you can make improvements. Consult with legal professionals or compliance experts to ensure that your company's practices regarding email marketing are in accordance with all laws and regulations that are currently in effect.

To summarize, maintaining compliance with the regulations governing email marketing is essential for the protection of your company as well as the preservation of the trust and confidence of your audience. You can ensure that your email marketing practices are ethical, transparent, and effective by complying with regulations such as the CAN-SPAM Act, the GDPR, and CASL and implementing best practices for staying compliant.

Chapter 21: Nurturing Your Subscribers and Building Trust

The development of long-term relationships with your target audience and the acceleration of conversions are both dependent on your ability to care for your email subscribers. You can build a loyal following and create advocates for your brand by delivering value to your subscribers, establishing trust with them, and maintaining consistent communication with them. In this chapter, we will discuss the most important strategies for fostering relationships with your subscribers and establishing credibility.

1. Provide Value

Providing consistent value to your subscribers through the content of your emails is one of the most important strategies for nurturing your subscriber relationships. These may take the form of entertaining content, educational resources, helpful hints and recommendations, exclusive offers and promotions, or any combination of these. You can demonstrate both your expertise and your dedication to the goal of providing value to your audience if you consistently provide value to them.

2. Segment Your Audience

It is possible to effectively target different groups of subscribers by segmenting your audience according to their interests, behaviors, and preferences. This can help you to engage with different groups of subscribers. You can improve engagement with your subscribers and build stronger relationships with them if you send content that is targeted to each segment and is personalized for that segment.

3. Communicate with One Another and One Another with You

It is a powerful method for fostering a sense of community and building trust with your subscribers if you engage in communication with them in two directions. Encourage your subscribers to respond to your emails, ask questions, and share their feedback and opinions by providing responses and sharing their thoughts. You can build a stronger connection with your subscribers and create advocates for your brand if you actively engage in conversation with them.

4. Be Consistent

When it comes to cultivating relationships with the people who have subscribed to your email list, consistency is essential. You can establish credibility with your audience and show them that you can be relied upon and committed to them if you send them high-quality content on a consistent basis and at regular intervals. This has the potential to help drive conversions and increase levels of engagement over time.

5. Make your communications more personal.

Personalizing your email communications with your subscribers can help them feel more valued and appreciated in your community. This may involve addressing the recipient by their first name in the emails you send them, making references to the customer's previous interactions with your brand, or sending personalized recommendations based on the customer's preferences or actions.

6. Make the Most of Content Generated by Users

Utilizing user-generated content, such as reviews left by previous customers or posts made on social media, is an effective method for establishing credibility and garnering social proof. You can demonstrate the value and satisfaction that your customers have experienced with your brand by featuring user-generated content in your email campaigns.

7. Be sure to provide outstanding service to your customers

It is essential to provide excellent customer service if you want to build trust with your subscribers and maintain relationships with them over the long term. This includes responding quickly to customer inquiries, addressing concerns and complaints raised by customers, and providing support that is both helpful and courteous.

THE LIST ADVANTAGE: UNLOCKING THE POWER OF LIST BUILDING FOR MARKETING SUCCESS

It is essential to adopt a holistic strategy for your email marketing in order to effectively nurture your email subscribers and build trust. Think about putting in place a program for the nurturing of leads that includes targeted and personalized email communication, in addition to other channels such as social media and customer service. This would be a good idea. Tracking engagement and conversions with the help of data and analytics is an effective way to continuously improve your email marketing strategy over time.

In conclusion, it is essential to build long-term relationships with your audience and to drive conversions by properly tending to your email subscribers as well as establishing trust between you and them. You can effectively nurture your subscribers and create brand advocates by consistently providing value, segmenting your audience, engaging in two-way communication, being consistent, personalizing your communication, leveraging user-generated content, and providing excellent customer service. In addition, you can increase the likelihood that your subscribers will recommend your brand to others.

Chapter 22: Leveraging Analytics to Improve Your List Building

When it comes to email marketing, analytics play an important part because they provide valuable insights into the performance of your campaigns as well as the behavior of your subscribers. Utilizing analytics allows you to pinpoint problem areas, enhance the performance of your email marketing campaigns, and, as a result, increase the effectiveness of your list-building efforts. In this chapter, we will discuss the most important analytics to monitor as well as how to make use of them to improve your list building.

1. The Sources of Traffic

It is essential to understand how visitors are discovering your content and interacting with it in order to understand how important it is to track the sources of traffic to your website and opt-in forms. You can determine which channels are the most effective at driving traffic to your website and opt-in forms by conducting an analysis of the traffic sources, and then you can adjust your marketing efforts in accordance with those findings.

2. Rates of Successful Conversion

It is essential to monitor the conversion rates of your opt-in forms, landing pages, and lead magnets in order to gain an understanding of how effective they are. You can determine which aspects of your strategy for list building are most effective at persuading visitors to sign up for your email list and then optimize those aspects in accordance with your findings from the analysis of your conversion rates.

3. The Probability of Giving Up

The term "abandonment rates" refers to the proportion of site visitors who start filling out an opt-in form but do not go on to finish it. Monitoring the rates at which users give up during the sign-up process can assist you in locating potential roadblocks or challenges in the process so that you can implement changes to reduce drop-offs and improve conversions.

4. Rates of Participation in Email

Monitoring the engagement rates of your email campaigns, such as the open rates, click-through rates, and conversion rates, can provide extremely helpful information regarding the efficiency of your email marketing efforts. You can determine which emails are most successful at engaging subscribers and driving conversions by analyzing these rates, and then you can adjust the content of your emails and the calls to action in accordance with that information.

5. The demographics of the subscribers

Monitoring subscriber demographics like age, gender, location, and interests can give you valuable insights into your audience and help you formulate a strategy for list building. You will be able to determine which segments of your audience are the most engaged with your brand and tailor your marketing efforts to appeal to those segments if you conduct a demographic analysis of your subscribers.

6. Activities of Subscribers

When you track the behavior of your subscribers, such as their engagement with your emails, their purchase history, and their activity on your website, you can gain valuable insights into the preferences and interests of your audience. You can identify opportunities for cross-selling and up-selling, as well as personalized marketing efforts to improve subscriber engagement and loyalty, by analyzing the behavior of your subscribers.

It is important to keep track of these key metrics over time and use them to inform your marketing strategy if you want to effectively leverage analytics to improve the effectiveness of your efforts to build your list. You should think about conducting A/B tests to test various elements of your opt-in forms, landing pages, and email campaigns, and then track performance to determine which strategies for list building are the most effective. Make effective use of data and analytics to continually improve the effectiveness of your list-building efforts and drive consistent results.

In conclusion, leveraging analytics is essential if you want to improve your efforts to build your email list and drive results with your email marketing. You can gain valuable insights into the performance of your email marketing campaigns by tracking traffic sources, conversion rates, abandonment rates, email engagement rates, subscriber demographics, and subscriber behavior. This allows you to optimize your list building strategy in a manner that is congruent with these newfound understandings. Make use of data and analytics to continuously test and improve the effectiveness of your list-building efforts, which will ultimately lead to success in email marketing over the long term.

Chapter 23: Tapping into the Power of Mobile List Building

Accessing the internet and viewing content is increasingly moving to mobile devices, which are becoming the primary means for doing so. As a consequence of this, it is imperative for companies to place a high priority on mobile optimization as part of their strategy for list building. You will be able to effectively reach and engage with your mobile audience as well as drive conversions if you take advantage of the power of mobile list building. In this chapter, we will discuss the most important techniques for constructing mobile mailing lists.

1. Landing Pages that Are Optimized for Mobile Devices

Landing pages that are optimized for mobile devices are necessary in order to engage with your mobile audience and increase conversions. Landing pages that are optimized for mobile devices are created to be responsive and load quickly on mobile devices. This makes it simple for site visitors to sign up for your email list. Simplify your landing pages as much as possible by removing any text or visual elements that aren't necessary, and check to see that your opt-in form can be seen clearly and is easily accessed using a mobile device.

2. SMS Marketing

SMS marketing is an effective method that can be used to engage with your mobile audience and encourage people to sign up for your email list. You can encourage mobile users to sign up for your email list and receive even more valuable content and offers by providing an incentive in the form of exclusive promotions, discounts, or content that is only accessible via SMS. Make sure that you comply with the regulations that govern SMS marketing, such as obtaining the subscribers' express consent before sending them marketing messages.

3. Opt-in Forms that Are Mobile-Friendly

Forms of opt-in that are designed specifically for use on mobile devices are absolutely necessary in order to successfully engage with your mobile audience. Make sure to use fonts that are large and simple to read, and keep the text on your opt-in forms brief and to the point. Reduce the amount of friction in your opt-in form by limiting the number of fields and making it as simple as possible for mobile users to register for your email list.

4. Mobile-Responsive Emails

Emails that are responsive to mobile devices are necessary if you want to engage with your mobile audience and make certain that your content can be accessed and read without difficulty on mobile devices. Optimize the content of your emails by using short, concise subject lines and by breaking up your content into easily digestible chunks. Email templates that are mobile-responsive can automatically adjust to fit the screen size of your audience when they are using their mobile devices.

5. Social Media Ads that Are Compatible with Mobile Devices

Advertisements on social media platforms that are tailored specifically for mobile use have the potential to be an efficient method of not only reaching and engaging with your mobile audience but also driving sign-ups for your email list. When trying to convince mobile users to sign up for your email list, you should use messaging that is direct and to the point, as well as visuals that grab their attention, and forceful calls to action.

6. Lead Magnets that Are Compatible with Mobile Devices

Motivating mobile users to sign up for your email list through the use of lead magnets that are optimized for mobile devices can be an effective way to grow your subscriber base. You might want to think about providing lead magnets that are mobile-only and exclusive, such as mobile app downloads, exclusive promotions, or content that is mobile-friendly.

It is essential to give mobile optimization a high priority in your email marketing strategy if you want to effectively capitalize on the power of mobile list building. It is a good idea to conduct user testing to ensure that all of your mobile-friendly content, including opt-in forms, landing pages, emails, and lead magnets, is optimized for use on mobile devices. Maintain a close eye on your analytics to keep tabs on how well your mobile list-building efforts are performing, and make it a point to continually improve your mobile marketing strategies as time goes on.

In conclusion, building a mobile list is necessary if you want to effectively engage with your mobile audience and drive conversions. You will be able to effectively reach and engage with your mobile audience as well as build a loyal following over time if you prioritize mobile optimization in your landing pages, opt-in forms, emails, social media ads, and lead magnets. Make use of data and analytics to monitor how well your mobile list building efforts are performing, and make sure to continuously improve your mobile marketing strategies to ensure your business's continued success.

Chapter 24: The Benefits of List Building for E-commerce Businesses

Building a customer list is an essential component of any e-commerce company's marketing strategy if they want to expand their customer base and boost their sales. E-commerce businesses have the ability to effectively promote their products, drive traffic to their website, and ultimately increase revenue if they construct an email list of subscribers who are engaged and interested in the subject matter. In this chapter, we will discuss the most important advantages that list building can provide for e-commerce companies.

1. An increase in overall sales

E-commerce companies can boost their sales with the help of list building because it provides a direct line of communication with subscribers who are interested and engaged in the business. You can promote your products and drive traffic to your website by sending targeted and personalized email campaigns to the recipients on your email list. This will ultimately lead to an increase in sales and revenue.

2. Promotion of Repeat Business Email marketing is an effective tool for fostering customer loyalty and encouraging repeat business among an existing customer base. You can incentivize customers to make repeat purchases and foster a sense of loyalty to your brand by sending personalized and targeted email campaigns to your email list. Incentives like this can be used to encourage customers to buy from you more than once.

3. Marketing that is Efficient in Terms of Cost

Email marketing is a cost-effective marketing strategy for e-commerce businesses because it requires a minimal investment in terms of both resources and budget. This makes email marketing one of the most popular marketing methods. E-commerce businesses can effectively reach their target audience without breaking the bank if they build an email list and send email campaigns that are targeted and personalized.

4. Data-Driven Marketing

E-commerce businesses have the ability to collect valuable data on their subscribers through the process of list building, and then use this data to inform their marketing strategy. E-commerce businesses can gain valuable insights into the preferences and behaviors of their audience by tracking the engagement on their emails, the activity on their websites, and their purchase histories. These businesses can then use this data to inform their marketing efforts.

5. Establishing a Strong Online Presence and Building Your Brand

Email marketing is an effective tool for establishing a strong online presence and building your brand. E-commerce companies can cultivate a devoted customer base and establish themselves as authorities in their field by sending out emails that are regularly updated with content that is both informative and interesting.

6. Marketing Tailored to the Individual

E-commerce companies can personalize their marketing efforts and provide a tailored experience to each subscriber by developing their subscriber lists through list building. You will be able to effectively target and engage with different groups of subscribers if you segment your email list based on the interests, behaviors, and preferences of your subscribers. Additionally, you will be able to provide a personalized experience that will drive engagement and loyalty.

7. Strengthened Connections with Our Clientele

Marketing via email is an effective tool for strengthening relationships with existing customers and fostering a sense of community among target audience members. E-commerce businesses have the ability to build strong relationships with their customers, which can foster a sense of loyalty and advocacy on their behalf. This can be accomplished by engaging in two-way communication with their subscribers, providing a prompt response to customer inquiries, and providing excellent customer service.

It is essential to adopt a comprehensive strategy for email marketing if you wish for your e-commerce company to reap the benefits of list building to the fullest extent possible. Think about putting in place lead nurturing programs that involve targeted and individualized email communication, in addition to other channels like social media and customer service. Tracking engagement and conversions with the help of data and analytics is an effective way to continuously improve your email marketing strategy over time.

List building is an essential marketing strategy for e-commerce businesses that want to increase sales, foster loyalty, and build a strong online presence. In conclusion, e-commerce businesses should prioritize list building. E-commerce businesses are able to effectively reach and engage with their target audience and drive long-term success by leveraging the benefits of list building, such as increased sales, repeat business, cost-effective marketing, data-driven marketing, brand building, personalized marketing, and improved customer relationships. List building also helps businesses build their brand. Make effective use of data and analytics to continually improve the effectiveness of your list-building efforts and drive consistent results.

Chapter 25: Implementing List Building for B2B Marketing Success

Building a customer list is a crucial component of any B2B marketing strategy that seeks to expand the clientele of the company, boost annual revenue, and solidify its position as a dominant player online. Businesses that sell to other businesses can effectively reach and engage with their target audience, drive traffic to their website, and ultimately increase sales by compiling an email list of subscribers who are interested and engaged in the brand's offerings. In this chapter, we will discuss the key strategies that should be implemented when building a list in order to achieve success in B2B marketing.

1. Create Valuable Content

It is essential to create content that is both valuable and engaging, that speaks to the needs and interests of your target audience, in order to effectively build an email list for the purposes of B2B marketing success. Consider producing thought leadership content such as white papers, case studies, industry reports, and other types of content that, when read by your target audience, will provide them with insightful knowledge and information of value. You can create an incentive for potential subscribers to sign up for your email list and engage with your brand by providing content that is of value to them.

2. Use Lead Magnets

The use of lead magnets is an effective and efficient method for encouraging prospective subscribers to sign up for your email list. You might want to think about offering exclusive content in exchange for email sign-ups. Some examples of this include industry reports, white papers, and eBooks. You can effectively build your email list and drive engagement with your target audience by offering valuable content in exchange for email sign-ups. This strategy is called a content exchange.

3. Optimize Your Website If you want to effectively engage with your target audience and drive conversions, optimizing your website so that you can build a list of email subscribers is essential. You should make sure to include prominent opt-in forms on your website, and you should also consider using pop-up forms or exit-intent forms to capture the attention of potential subscribers. In order to effectively engage with people using mobile devices, you need to ensure that the opt-in forms on your website are easy to find and navigate, and that your website is optimized for use on mobile devices.

4. Make Your Marketing More Personalized

When it comes to effectively engaging with your B2B audience and driving conversions, personalization is an absolute necessity. You will be able to effectively target and engage with different groups of subscribers if you segment your email list based on the interests, behaviors, and preferences of your subscribers. Additionally, you will be able to provide a personalized experience that will drive engagement and loyalty.

5. Make use of social media platforms.

The success of business-to-business (B2B) marketing can be greatly aided by the utilization of social media as an effective tool. Think about establishing connections with potential subscribers and promoting your email list by utilizing social media platforms such as LinkedIn. Make sure that your social media profiles are optimized, that you are sending targeted messages, and that you are engaging with your audience in order to increase audience participation and build your email list.

6. Implement Lead Nurturing

The success of B2B list building and marketing is directly correlated to the quality of the leads that are nurtured. You might want to think about putting in place automated lead nurturing programs that provide potential subscribers with email communication that is both targeted and personalized. Make use of data and analytics to

THE LIST ADVANTAGE: UNLOCKING THE POWER OF LIST BUILDING FOR MARKETING SUCCESS

monitor the rates of engagement and conversion in order to continuously improve the effectiveness of your lead nurturing over time.

It is important to take a holistic approach to your marketing strategy if you want to effectively implement list building for the success of your business-to-business (B2B) marketing. You should think about incorporating a variety of lead magnets, website optimization, personalized marketing, social media promotion, and lead nurturing into your strategy. Additionally, you should use data and analytics to track engagement and conversions over the course of time.

List building is an essential marketing strategy for B2B companies that want to grow their customer base, increase revenue, and establish a strong online presence, all of which can be accomplished through the use of the strategy. B2B companies can effectively build their email list and drive long-term success by implementing strategies such as creating valuable content, utilizing lead magnets, optimizing their website, personalizing their marketing, leveraging social media, and implementing lead nurturing. Make effective use of data and analytics to continually improve the effectiveness of your list-building efforts and drive consistent results.

Chapter 26: Scaling Your List Building Efforts for Rapid Growth

It is essential to scale your list building efforts in order to achieve rapid growth in your email list and sustained success in the long term. You will be able to effectively reach and engage with your target audience, which will ultimately lead to increased revenue and growth if you put into practice effective strategies for list building and scale your efforts over time. In this chapter, we will discuss the most important strategies for accelerating the growth of your mailing list in order to scale your list building efforts.

1. Place your emphasis on quality.

When it comes to compiling a list, the quality of the entries is more important than the quantity of them. Instead of concentrating solely on rapidly expanding the size of your email list, you should work on constructing a list of subscribers who are actively engaged in your content and interested in receiving it. You can effectively reach and engage with the people in your target audience, as well as drive long-term success, if you concentrate on quality.

2. Use Multiple Channels

It is essential to use multiple channels to reach and engage with your target audience if you want to effectively scale the list building efforts you are undertaking. If you want to effectively promote your email list and reach potential subscribers, you should think about utilizing social media, lead magnets, website optimization, paid advertising, and any number of other channels.

3. Make the Most of Partnerships

Establishing strategic alliances can be an effective way to scale your list-building efforts and propel rapid expansion. To effectively promote your email list and get in front of a larger audience, you should think about forming strategic partnerships with industry influencers, brands, or other businesses. You will be able to effectively build your email list, which will drive increased engagement and revenue if you leverage partnerships.

4. Use Paid Advertising

Paid advertising has the potential to be a powerful tool that can help you scale your list building efforts and drive rapid growth. If you want to effectively promote your email list and reach potential subscribers, you might want to take into consideration using advertising platforms such as Google Ads, Facebook Ads, or LinkedIn Ads. Make sure to use messaging that is targeted, and optimize your campaigns so that they generate the most engagement and conversions possible.

5. Optimisation de votre site Internet Optimisation de votre site Internet for the purpose of list building is essential if you want to scale your efforts effectively and drive rapid growth. You should make sure to include prominent opt-in forms on your website, and you should also consider using pop-up forms or exit-intent forms to capture the attention of potential subscribers. To effectively engage with people using mobile devices, you need to ensure that the opt-in forms on your website are easy to find and navigate, and that your website is optimized for use on mobile devices.

6. Make Use of Marketing Through Referrals

Referral marketing is an effective strategy that can scale the list-building efforts you put in place and drive rapid growth. Consider putting in place a referral program that provides subscribers with an incentive for inviting their friends and family members to join your email list. You can effectively build your email list and drive increased engagement and revenue by offering referral bonuses and rewards to your customers.

7. Carry out ongoing testing and improvements.

It is essential to continually test and optimize your strategies over time in order to scale the effectiveness of your list building efforts and drive rapid growth. Tracking engagement and conversion rates can be done with the help of data and analytics; then, adjust your strategies based on the findings to achieve the best possible results. Make it a point to test out a variety of distribution methods, messages, and rewards in order to sustainably enhance your list-building activities and propel your business toward sustained success.

In conclusion, expanding the scope of your list building efforts is critical for achieving rapid expansion of your email list and sustained success over the long term. You can effectively scale your list building efforts and drive rapid growth by implementing effective strategies such as focusing on quality, utilizing multiple channels, leveraging partnerships, utilizing paid advertising, optimizing your website, utilizing referral marketing, and continuously testing and optimizing your strategies. Make effective use of data and analytics to continually improve the effectiveness of your list-building efforts and drive consistent results.

Chapter 27: Overcoming Common List Building Challenges

Building a list can be a challenging and complex process, and many businesses face common challenges when trying to build and grow their email list. One of these challenges is the ability to attract new subscribers. You will be able to effectively build a high-quality email list and drive long-term success if you understand and overcome the challenges that are presented here. In this chapter, we will discuss some of the more common difficulties that can arise when creating a list, as well as offer some solutions to these problems.

1. Low Rates of Volunteering to Participate

A low percentage of people opting in is one of the most common problems that arise when building email lists. If potential subscribers are not opting in to your email list, it can be difficult to build and grow your list in an effective manner over time. Consider implementing strategies such as improving the design of your opt-in form, optimizing your website for mobile devices, making use of lead magnets, and personalizing your messaging in order to effectively encourage potential subscribers to sign up for your email list. This will help you overcome the challenge that you are facing.

2. The Poor Quality of the Lead

Another common difficulty with list building is dealing with low-quality leads. It may be difficult to effectively communicate with and engage with your target audience if your email list is populated with subscribers who do not engage with your content or who are not interested in it. Consider putting into practice strategies such as personalizing the content of your messages, segmenting your email list according to the interests and actions of subscribers, and regularly cleaning your email list to remove inactive subscribers as a means of overcoming this obstacle.

3. Complaints Regarding Spam

Complaints about spam can be a significant obstacle to overcome when building a mailing list because they can have a detrimental effect on your sender reputation and lessen the efficiency of your email marketing campaigns. It is essential to ensure that your email marketing campaigns are in compliance with the industry regulations and that you are only sending emails to subscribers who have expressly opted in to receive them in order to be successful in overcoming this challenge. Be sure to monitor the metrics of your email campaign on a regular basis, and be sure to respond quickly to any issues or complaints that may arise.

4. Low Engagement Rates

Low engagement rates are a common challenge that can arise when building a list. This is because low engagement rates may indicate that your email marketing campaigns are not successfully reaching or engaging with the audience you want to reach. Consider putting into action strategies such as personalizing your messaging, segmenting your email list, routinely sending valuable and engaging content, and experimenting with various types of email campaigns, such as drip campaigns or targeted promotions, in order to overcome this obstacle.

5. A high rate of unsubscriptions

Because they may suggest that your email campaigns are not effectively engaging with your target audience or providing value to your subscribers, high unsubscribe rates can be a major challenge for list building. This is because high unsubscribe rates can indicate that your email campaigns are not engaging effectively with your target audience. Consider implementing strategies such as segmenting your email list based on the interests and behaviors of subscribers, personalizing your messaging, regularly sending valuable and engaging content, and regularly cleaning your email list to remove inactive subscribers so as to overcome this challenge. These strategies can be helpful in overcoming this obstacle.

6. Uneven and Unreliable Growth

Inconsistent growth can be a challenge for list building because it can be difficult to effectively grow your email list and drive long-term success without consistent growth. Inconsistent growth can also make it more difficult to measure growth over time. Consider putting into action strategies such as using multiple channels to promote your email list, regularly optimizing your website and opt-in forms, and experimenting with various types of lead magnets or incentives to encourage sign-ups in order to get around this obstacle.

In conclusion, the process of building a list can be difficult and complex; however, if you understand and are able to overcome common challenges such as low opt-in rates, poor lead quality, spam complaints, low engagement rates, high unsubscribe rates, and inconsistent growth, you will be able to build an effective high-quality email list that will drive long-term success. For the best possible outcomes, you must ensure that your strategies are continually tested and improved over time, and that you make use of data and analytics to monitor engagement and conversion rates.

Chapter 28: The Future of List Building and Email Marketing

List building and email marketing have been around for decades, but they are still developing new features and adapting to new technologies as well as shifting patterns of behavior among consumers. When we consider the future, it is abundantly clear that developing email lists and conducting email marketing will continue to be two of the most important tools for companies of any size to use in order to successfully communicate with and interact with the demographics of their choice. In this chapter, we will investigate the foreseeable future of list building and email marketing, as well as the trends that will continue to shape the evolution of these two marketing strategies.

1. An increased focus on individualization and customization

In recent years, personalization has garnered more and more attention, and it is expected that it will continue to be a major trend in list building and email marketing in the years to come. Businesses are able to effectively reach and engage with their target audience, as well as drive increased engagement and revenue, by utilizing data and analytics to segment their email lists and personalize the messaging they send.

2. The Persistent Expansion of Mobile

Mobile devices have quickly become an integral part of our day-to-day lives, and it is anticipated that they will continue to play a significant part in the development of email marketing strategies in the years to come. In order for businesses to effectively reach mobile users and engage with them, email marketing campaigns will need to be optimized for mobile devices. Additionally, mobile-specific strategies, such as push notifications and SMS messaging, will need to be utilized.

3. Incorporation of Additional Distribution Channels

The creation of email marketing lists and their integration with other marketing channels, such as social media and text message marketing, are both on the rise. Businesses are able to effectively build their email lists, which drives increased engagement and revenue, when they use multiple channels to reach and engage with their target audience as well as other audiences.

4. A.I. and ML (Machine Learning and Artificial Intelligence)

The use of artificial intelligence and machine learning will become increasingly prevalent in list building and email marketing in order to automate and improve the effectiveness of campaigns. Businesses are able to effectively reach and engage with their target audience, which drives increased engagement and revenue. This is made possible by utilizing tools powered by AI to analyze data and predict the behaviors of subscribers.

5. Greater Emphasis on Data Privacy In the recent years, data privacy has become a major concern, and it will continue to be a major trend in list building and email marketing in the years to come. Businesses will need to take steps to ensure that they are in compliance with industry regulations such as the General Data Protection Regulation (GDPR) and the California Consumer Privacy Act (CCPA), and that they are transparent and forthright with their customers and subscribers regarding the use of their data.

6. Place a Greater Emphasis on Metrics Relating to Engagement

In the years to come, list building and email marketing will still require the utilization of engagement metrics such as open rates, click-through rates, and conversion rates. Businesses are able to continuously optimize their email marketing campaigns and drive increased engagement and revenue when they make use of data and analytics to monitor engagement metrics.

7. The Implementation of Interactive Content

It is expected that interactive content such as quizzes, surveys, and polls will be used more frequently in list building and email marketing in order to generate higher levels of engagement and revenue. Businesses have the ability to more effectively reach and engage with

THE LIST ADVANTAGE: UNLOCKING THE POWER OF LIST BUILDING FOR MARKETING SUCCESS

their target audience, as well as drive increased engagement and revenue, by utilizing content that is interactive.

In conclusion, developing a mailing list and engaging in email marketing will remain two of the most important tools for companies of any size to use in order to effectively communicate with and interact with the demographics of their choice. Businesses are able to effectively build their email list and drive increased engagement and revenue by adapting to trends such as an increased emphasis on personalization, the continued growth of mobile, integration with other channels, artificial intelligence and machine learning, an increased focus on data privacy, a greater emphasis on engagement metrics, and the use of interactive content. For the best possible outcomes, you must ensure that your strategies are continually tested and improved over time, and that you make use of data and analytics to monitor engagement and conversion rates.

Also by B. Vincent

Affiliate Marketing
Affiliate Marketing
Affiliate Marketing

Standalone
Business Employee Discipline
Affiliate Recruiting
Business Layoffs & Firings
Business and Entrepreneur Guide
Business Remote Workforce
Career Transition
Project Management
Precision Targeting
Professional Development
Strategic Planning
Content Marketing
Imminent List Building
Getting Past GateKeepers
Banner Ads
Bookkeeping
Bridge Pages
Business Acquisition

Business Bogging
Business Communication Course
Marketing Automation
Better Meetings
Business Conflict Resolution
Business Culture Course
Conversion Optimization
Creative Solutions
Employee Recruitment
Startup Capital
Employee Incentives
Employee Mentoring
Followership
Servant Leadership
Human Resources
Team Building
Freelancing
Funnel Building
Geo Targeting
Goal Setting
Immanent List Building
Lead Generation
Leadership Course
Leadership Transition
Leadership vs Management
LinkedIn Ads
LinkedIn Marketing
Messenger Marketing
New Management
Newsfeed Ads
Search Ads
Online Learning
Sales Webinars

Side Hustles
Split Testing
Twitter Timeline Advertising
Earning Additional Income Through Side Hustles: Begin Earning Money Immediately
Making a Living Through Blogging: Earn Money Working From Home
Create Bonuses for Affiliate Marketing: Your Success Is Encompassed by Your Bonuses
Internet Marketing Success: The Most Effective Traffic-Driving Strategies
JV Recruiting: Joint Ventures Partnerships and Affiliates
Secrets to List Building
Step-by-Step Facebook Marketing: Discover How To Create A Strategy That Will Help You Grow Your Business
Banner Advertising: Traffic Can Be Boosted by Banner Ads
Affiliate Marketing
Improve Your Marketing Strategy with Internet Marketing
Outsourcing Helps You Save Time and Money
Choosing the Right Content and Marketing for Social Media
Make Products That Will Sell
Launching a Product for Affiliate Marketing
Pinterest as a Marketing Tool
The List Advantage: Unlocking the Power of List Building for Marketing Success

About the Publisher

Accepting manuscripts in the most categories. We love to help people get their words available to the world.

Revival Waves of Glory focus is to provide more options to be published. We do traditional paperbacks, hardcovers, audio books and ebooks all over the world. A traditional royalty-based publisher that offers self-publishing options, Revival Waves provides a very author friendly and transparent publishing process, with President Bill Vincent involved in the full process of your book. Send us your manuscript and we will contact you as soon as possible.

Contact: Bill Vincent at rwgpublishing@yahoo.com

www.ingramcontent.com/pod-product-compliance
Lightning Source LLC
LaVergne TN
LVHW091558060526
838200LV00036B/895